IDEAS TO GO

SELF-ESTEEM

Ages 6-8

Activities and ideas to develop children's self-esteem,
across the Curriculum

Tanya Dalgleish

A & C Black • Londo

CONTENTS

INTRODUCTION

Good self-esteem has been shown to be vitally important for children's happiness, social and emotional well-being, and academic success. Mental health and well-being are key themes of the National Healthy Schools Programme, launched in 1999, which encourages schools to play a part in improving children's health. This book provides teachers with ideas and activities to help pupils develop their self-esteem. The activities make an ideal complement to classroom work across the Curriculum. They can be used in isolation, in sequence, or dipped into, as teachers require. The activities will help children to value themselves as individuals and to value the individuality of others, while appreciating concepts such as co-operation, negotiation and tolerance.

ABOUT THIS BOOK

TEACHERS' FILE

The teachers' file offers advice on how to make the most of this book. It offers ideas for classroom organisation as well as ICT tips, assessment ideas and suggestions for parental involvement.

QUICK STARTS

This section offers activity and game ideas that help to promote children's self-esteem. The activities require little or no preparation and can be used across various learning areas to complement existing lesson plans.

ACTIVITY BANK

The activity bank contains 28 photocopiable activities which cover five topic areas: valuing self; valuing others; feelings and emotions; strengths and limitations; and likes and dislikes. The activities can be used in any order and can be adapted to suit individual pupils or classes.

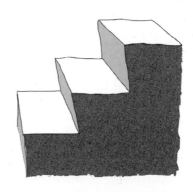

Photocopiable activities

CHALLENGES

These photocopiable task cards offer creative investigational challenges. They can be given to individual pupils or groups, and they can be used at any time and in any order. The task cards are aimed at Key Stage 2 pupils and more able pupils in Key Stage 1, as they require pupils to follow instructions and complete a task independently.

HOW TO USE THIS BOOK

QUICK STARTS

Quick starts are ideal warm-up activities for the beginning of a lesson. Each activity is intended to provide 10–15 minutes of group or whole class discussion. Reflect on the completed task with the children. Ask what they learned and whether there was anything that surprised them.

Example How would you feel? (page 13) is ideal to open discussions about feelings. It gives children the opportunity to consider complex feelings through a third person.

How would you feel?

Have pupils take on roles of other children in various situations, or of characters in literature. (How did the three bears feel when they found Goldilocks in their house? How would you feel if you got home from school and found a stranger had eaten your food and broken your things and was asleep in your bed?)

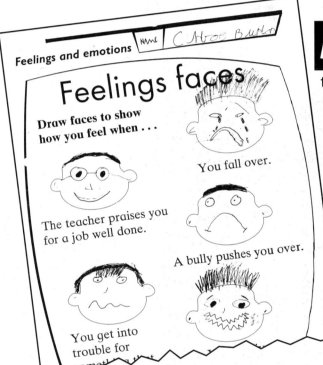

Feelings and emotions   NAME Carol Burton

Feelings faces

Draw faces to show how you feel when . . .

The teacher praises you for a job well done.

You fall over.

A bully pushes you over.

You get into trouble for something that

ACTIVITY BANK

These photocopiable activities can be used by individuals, groups or the whole class. They could provide the focus for a whole lesson. The activities will not in themselves achieve the objectives, but they will make children start to think about these very complex issues. Many of the activities touch on sensitive issues, particularly for pupils with low self-esteem; take this into consideration when introducing the activities and discussing outcomes. It is helpful to make it clear to pupils whether the activity is to be private or shared, especially for pupils at the top end of Key Stage 2.

Example Feelings faces (page 35) allows children to express particular feelings in a visual way. Extend the discussion to include the effect our own feelings may have on others.

CHALLENGES

These photocopiable activities are perfect for use in learning centres, in the school library or in the classroom. The investigational nature of the activities is in line with National Curriculum requirements and supports the development of investigational problem-solving skills.

Example Me mobiles (page 46) will give teachers a good insight into each child's level of self-esteem. Children could try different structures for their mobiles, and discuss the relative benefits of each. They could also use a varying number of attachments.

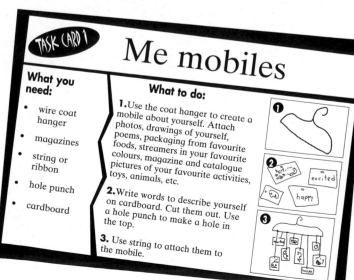

TASK CARD 1

Me mobiles

What you need:

- wire coat hanger
- magazines
- string or ribbon
- hole punch
- cardboard

What to do:

1. Use the coat hanger to create a mobile about yourself. Attach photos, drawings of yourself, poems, packaging from favourite foods, streamers in your favourite colours, magazine and catalogue pictures of your favourite activities, toys, animals, etc.

2. Write words to describe yourself on cardboard. Cut them out. Use a hole punch to make a hole in the top.

3. Use string to attach them to the mobile.

TEACHERS' FILE

ABOUT SELF-ESTEEM

Motivation

The most important form of motivation is intrinsic motivation, which comes from within the child instead of being aimed at external reward or praise. Children who feel good about themselves are intrinsically motivated. They are more likely to be successful. For example, pupils who feel good about their reading ability choose to read and therefore become better readers. Success in one area allows pupils to be risk-takers and triers in other areas. The key for the teacher is to find an area in which the pupil excels and use that success as a springboard for other successes. Teachers can use a survey to find out about children's interests and other things they may be good at.

What is Self-esteem?

Self-esteem means how we feel about ourselves. For a child, self-esteem can involve: how you think you are regarded by your family, teachers and classmates; how you feel about yourself as a pupil or as a friend; whether you think other pupils like you or not; and how effective you feel you are in managing your life. Children who feel 'different' tend to have lower self-esteem. If children have negative feelings about themselves, they are more likely to display negative feelings towards others, to underachieve in school, and to develop behavioural problems and/or anti-social behaviour.

Early childhood is the optimum time to foster self-esteem in children; the older a child becomes, the harder it is to counter the effects of low self-esteem. It is important to help pupils maintain a balanced view of themselves, which includes recognising and valuing their own strengths while accepting their limitations. Encourage pupils to set realistic goals. Simply 'to be the best you can be' is a worthwhile goal. If teachers encourage pupils to value themselves as individuals and to value the individuality of others, while reinforcing the importance of co-operation and tolerance, pupils will develop a positive, optimistic outlook on life.

Friendship

It is vital for children's self-esteem for them to feel that they are accepted by their teachers and classmates. Help children to understand that they don't have to like or be liked by everyone, but they do need to accept and be accepted by others. You could model how to give and receive compliments, and demonstrate how you value and respect each child and his or her feelings.

Conflict resolution

Explain to pupils how they can try to resolve conflict. You could introduce children to the following process:
● Articulate the problem
● Discuss possible solutions
● Make a choice about a solution
● Reflect on the outcome

CLASSROOM ORGANISATION

How to use this book (page 4) suggests a range of approaches for using self-esteem activities in the classroom. The activities in this book could also be used in the following ways:

- For individuals during a wet playtime
- In small groups with a Learning Support Assistant
- As homework for a PSE lesson on a related theme
- As a focus for a circle time discussion for a small group
- For paired reading in Literacy
- For individuals working with parents or an older pupil

In promoting mutual respect, co-operation and individuality, it is also useful to consider the parts played by the classroom environment, accessibility of resources and classroom management.

The classroom environment

A supportive classroom environment makes pupils feel secure and helps them to face the challenges presented by school life. Children know that they will be listened to, their contributions will be valued and their opinions respected. It takes time to establish this kind of environment, but the benefits for teachers as well as pupils are worth the effort. The teacher should aim to put aside any personal feelings towards particular pupils and take positive steps to respect and value all pupils equally.

When something positive is achieved by the class, make the most of it by focusing pupils' attention on the achievement. Pupils could write the outcome on a chart for display, for example, 'We worked together to perform the class play' or 'We helped each other learn our spelling words'. Display pupils' work and allow opportunities for them to respond to each other's work, for example, 'I like that painting because I like the bright colours'. Help pupils to develop appropriate language and vocabulary for commenting on each other's work. If possible, ensure that something positive is said about each pupil's efforts.

At the end of every day, try to allow time for reflection. Reflection gives children time to think about what they have done, attempted or achieved. When given opportunities to reflect, pupils learn to recognise and take pleasure in what they have accomplished.

Ways to enhance the learning environment:
- Improve the classroom layout and use displays as visual stimuli
- Select teaching methods and organisational strategies appropriate to the pupils' needs
- Create a learning environment of high challenge and low stress
- Establish a positive, welcoming atmosphere
- Vary the way pupils work – for example, independently or in small groups
- Aim for a balance between structured and unstructured tasks
- Use a variety of learning styles – for example, hands on, visual, oral, written
- Establish the 'big picture' by linking tasks with pupils' experiences
- Use music to enhance the learning environment and to improve the children's ability to recall information

Co-operative learning

Co-operative learning activities encourage communication, collaboration and negotiation. They can lead to a deeper understanding of subject matter, higher self-esteem and greater self-confidence. Through sharing their skills, pupils learn that they are accepted by others and valued as group members. Co-operation can be encouraged through games and group activities such as multi-voice recitation, science experiments and so on. Aim to provide a balance of co-operative and independent activities. Some gifted pupils may become frustrated if they are always asked to work collaboratively; they need also to work on independent tasks that they can pursue at length and to the best of their abilities.

Bibliotherapy

Books can be used in the classroom to help pupils understand their own problems. Children often find it easy to identify and empathise with characters in literature, by relating the characters' situations to their own. Using literature in this way helps children to realise that there are other children in similar positions to themselves. They also learn that problems can be faced and usually solved. If you are aware of a pupil with a particular difficulty (for example, divorce in the family, death of a pet, sibling rivalry, disability, difficulty establishing or maintaining friendships, shyness or bullying), you could choose a relevant story for the children to read, showing tact and sensitivity about why that particular book is being read.

Self-esteem learning centres

A self-esteem learning centre could be set up in part of the classroom or as a shared resource for the whole school, perhaps in part of the school library. The learning centre might contain relevant books, jigsaw puzzles, maths equipment, construction blocks, a listening post, paper, pencils and a supply of art materials. It is a good idea to set up folders of blank worksheets and add new ones regularly. Provide a set of activity cards, some of which could be topic-based and some generic, for example, 'Research a favourite animal', 'Write a poem about your favourite food', 'Work in a group to conduct the following experiment', and so on. Provide activities that allow for both independent and group work. A computer is useful for encouraging pupils to use software collaboratively. You could also provide a book in which pupils can record discoveries or useful tips for pupils working there in future.

Grouping children

Grouping pupils in different ways allows for a variety of interactions amongst them. Groups may be homogeneous (pupils of similar abilities, interests or backgrounds) or heterogeneous (pupils of differing abilities, interests or backgrounds). Smaller groups generally work best because they allow all pupils to participate in the discussion. Pupils can be assigned roles within the group, such as 'recorder' and 'reporter'. The recorder makes notes of important points or decisions. The reporter's job is to report to the class on the group's discussion. The teacher can assign the roles or ask the group to decide who should do the jobs. Ensure that over time, every pupil has an opportunity to take on each of the roles.

Games

Games in which everyone co-operates and all pupils are winners can play a part in establishing a classroom environment that promotes pupils' self-esteem. Competition has a place, but in games where there are winners and losers, the loser may feel miserable. It is important to ensure that no pupil continually loses or is always picked last when forming teams.

ICT TIPS

ICT skills can be integrated into many aspects of learning. If computers are to become a valuable part of the classroom, it must be easy for children to use them independently. It can be a help to have a parent rota which arranges for a parent to sit at the computer with children and offer assistance when needed.

Choose software that provides opportunities for positive interaction between the children in a group, and between children and adults. Software can encourage problem-solving and the use of thinking skills, while including fun aspects such as music and animation. This will improve children's self-esteem by allowing them to solve problems, make decisions and work co-operatively with others. Avoid programs that require reading skills beyond the children's ability, or are too difficult for children to navigate, as these will lead to feelings of frustration and incompetence.

It is important to let pupils make mistakes along with their successes. Pupils will learn by trying things out on their own, and by talking about what worked and what did not. Be willing to listen to and discuss what students have done and what they have discovered.

Communication via e-mail can help to boost the confidence of students who are unsure of their communication skills, because there is no need for visual and non-verbal conversational cues. E-mail offers pupils the opportunity to correspond with a wide range of people as they develop their ICT skills. E-mail can be used in the classroom for various educational purposes. Activities could incorporate the following ideas:

Allow children to e-mail organisations such as charities to ask for information related to projects they are studying

Set up links with other classes and pupils so that children can collaborate on projects and lessons

Arrange for pupils to become e-pals with other pupils around the world

ASSESSMENT

Self-esteem can be assessed by observing students over time. The following questions may be useful for assessment.

- Are pupils willing to take risks in their work and play, for example by using approximate spellings?
- Are they confident enough to 'have a go'?
- Are they eager to try new experiences and challenges?
- Are they positive in their reactions to new experiences?
- Do they make friends easily?
- Can they set goals for themselves?

- Are they positive in their reactions to teacher expectations?
- Are they realistic in their expectations of themselves?
- Can they accept defeat?
- Are they willing to learn from their mistakes?
- How do they cope with problems and set-backs?
- Are they confident enough to contribute to class discussions?

Encourage pupils to assess their own work, which could involve keeping folders of their best or most enjoyable projects. The aim is for children to be intrinsically motivated to do their best. Learning to evaluate their own efforts allows them to rely on their own values rather than on outside judgements.

PARENTAL INVOLVEMENT

It is beneficial to explain to parents why self-esteem is important for children's academic success, their happiness, and their social and emotional well-being. Explain that children who have negative feelings about themselves are more likely to display negative feelings towards others and to underachieve in school. You could inform parents that you want the children to achieve the following goals:

- To value themselves as individuals
- To value the individuality of others
- To work with others co-operatively
- To learn negotiation skills
- To appreciate the value of tolerance
- To learn how to make effective decisions for themselves

Invite parents to participate in classroom activities by sharing their skills or knowledge with pupils. Encourage them to share aspects of their cultural backgrounds through activities such as cooking, language, art, music and dance. You could involve the class and parents in community-based events such as Senior Citizens Week.

Ask parents to support your efforts at home by allowing children to make everyday choices such as what the family will have for dinner. In this way parents can let children know that their opinions are valued and respected. Suggest that parents phrase ground rules positively rather than negatively, saying, for example, 'When your room is tidy you can watch television,' rather than, 'If you don't tidy your room you won't be allowed to watch television.'

QUICK STARTS

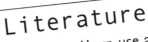

Literature

During the Literacy Hour, use a large book such as *A Huge Bag of Worries* by Virginia Ironside (Macdonald Young Books) for shared reading. Discuss the feelings of the characters and encourage pupils to feel empathy towards them. The children can then say whether the feelings relate to any situations in their own lives. Encourage them to explain their own feelings and how they deal with their problems.

Friendship stars

Write these words on the board.
- Honesty
- Sense of humour
- Kindness
- Good looks
- Helpfulness
- Intelligence
- Gentleness
- Popularity
- Generosity
- Loyalty

Ask pupils to decide which is the most important quality in a friend. Provide star templates so that each pupil can make a paper star and write their chosen word on it. Hang the friendship stars in the classroom.

Time lines

Have the children bring in photos of themselves as babies, toddlers and younger than they are now. Display them and discuss how they have grown and changed. Discuss what they would like to do when they grow older. List some of their hopes and goals. They could draw or make a collage from magazine pictures the things they hope to achieve, do, be and have. Encourage them to see beyond material possessions in their futures.

Extension: Ask staff at school to bring in their own baby photos and have a guessing competition for the whole school to match the correct baby photo with each teacher.

Puppets

Make puppets from lollipop sticks, wooden spoons, paper plates, socks, boxes or paper bags. Use them for pupils' own play-making, performances of scripted plays and adaptations of traditional stories such as *The Little Red Hen*.

Silhouettes

Use an OHP to create silhouettes of the pupils' profiles. Attach a sheet of chart paper to a wall. Have each pupil stand side-on against the wall. Use the OHP light to cast a silhouette of the pupil's face. Trace the silhouette on to the chart paper. Have the pupil paint the silhouette black and then write a label or poem to be displayed with it.

Make a class book

Have pupils write a recount of an excursion, or choose a theme (you could have pupils suggest themes and draw one out of a hat), and have each child write a story or poem about it. Have them decorate their stories/poems, and combine them into a class book. Make a title page for the book that names all the pupils as authors. Display the book somewhere that pupils have access to.

Postie!

Set up a classroom letterbox. Use a cardboard box with a slot cut out of it. Cover the box with red wrapping paper or red paint. Write Post Office on it in white lettering. Allow time each day for pupils to write letters to you, each other, other teachers and children in other classes. Allow time each day for a designated 'postie' to empty the box and deliver the mail. Allow time for pupils to reply to their post and post these letters for delivery the next day.

How would you feel?

Have pupils take on roles of other children in various situations, or of characters in literature. (How did the three bears feel when they found Goldilocks in their house? How would you feel if you got home from school and found a stranger had eaten your food and broken your things and was asleep in your bed?)

Hot potato

Have pupils sit in a circle on the floor and pass an object around the circle (tennis ball/rock/flower). As the children receive an object they say something nice about the person they are about to pass the object on to.

Variations: Compliment Circle
1. Pupils sit in a circle with one pupil in the middle who is not allowed to speak. All the pupils in the circle take turns to pay the pupil in the centre a compliment.
2. Pupils sit in a circle and a mirror is passed from one pupil to the next. As each pupil receives the mirror they must pay themselves a compliment.

Music, art and movement

Have pupils experiment with various musical instruments and consider how these sounds can express emotions. If no ready-made musical instruments are available, have pupils use classroom objects such as rulers, blackboard dusters and so on to create the sounds for the feelings. Give pupils art paper and mixed media and ask them to create a picture that expresses the same feelings as the sounds. Have pupils explore movement, body language and facial expression to express sounds or the feelings and emotions.

Variation: Use ready-made music and have pupils express the mood of the music through movement.

Where do you belong?

Allow the children to sort themselves into lines based on different criteria such as height (tallest to shortest), foot size (smallest to largest), hair length (shortest to longest), age (oldest to youngest) and so on. Pupils can suggest their own criteria. This gives different children opportunities to be first in line. Or have pupils get into groups based on various criteria such favourite animal, birth month, favourite TV show.

Musical gym mats

A variation of musical chairs which is non-competitive. Start with all the children standing on some gym mats (door mats or carpet squares work well too) in the centre of the room. Play music and have the children dance around the room. When the music stops all pupils need to stand on a mat. Take a mat away every time the music starts. The children must ensure that everyone can fit on to the mats. The game is over when a child can't fit on a mat.

A knotty situation

Have the children work in groups of five or six. Have them stand in a circle and hold hands with the children across the circle from them. Each child should be holding two other childrens' hands, and no child should hold the hand of the person beside them in the circle. Now tell the children to untangle themselves without letting go of the hands they are holding. As the children become more practised in untangling themselves you can work in larger groups.

Pupil of the Week

Randomly select a 'Pupil of the Week'. Set up a bulletin board display featuring the pupil of the week. Display photos of the student as well as portraits and self-portraits. Have everyone in the class write a positive message and display these as well. Choose this child to run errands and perform important duties for the week. Award a 'Pupil of the Week' certificate at the end of the week so that the pupil has something to take home.

Modelling

Have students work in pairs. One student uses the other as a model, and moulds their body into favourite food, favourite person, favourite book character, favourite television character and so on. Have students explain what they have created to the rest of the class and then swap roles.

Living sculptures

Have pupils work in groups to create sculptures. Tell them that you will call a number and that number dictates how many bases of support their group sculpture can have. Bases of support means parts of the body allowed to be touching the ground, e.g. three bases of support can mean two feet and one hand, or one knee, one hand and a foot, etc. The challenge is to create interesting sculptures as a group.

Tape recordings

Record pupils' stories and use the tapes for a listening post or in the activity centre. Pupils can record their own readings of their stories or the stories of others. Tape recorders can also be used to record multi-voice recitations, sound collage, experiments with music, and so on. Children love to hear their own voices and show great delight in listening to themselves.

Singing with attitude

Familiar songs, chants and poems such as 'Miss Polly had a Dolly' or 'Humpty Dumpty' can be sung or recited in voices that communicate different emotions. For example, they can be chanted, recited or sung sadly, happily, excitedly, with a surprised voice or angrily. Pupils can work in groups to organise and perform the recitations. They may also choose to dramatise the recitations.

Sound collage

Have students make sounds to accompany a story reading or telling, or the recitation of a poem. The sounds can be vocal sounds or body percussion. Students need to work together to decide on the appropriate sounds and their sequence.

Reflecting on the day

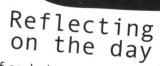

At the end of each day ask pupils what they learned during the day, what new things they found out, what they did well, what they need to learn to do better, who they helped and who helped them. Reinforce the positive aspects of the day. Help pupils think of something to tell parents about.

ACTIVITY BANK

NAME

About me

My name is _____.

My birthday is on _____.

I am _____ years old.

My favourite story is _____.

Things I can do:

1. _____

2. _____

3. _____

My family looks like this.
(Draw and label your family members.)

Helps identify individual characteristics and skills.

NAME

Fingerprints

Use an ink pad to take your fingerprints. No one else in the world has exactly the same fingerprints as you!

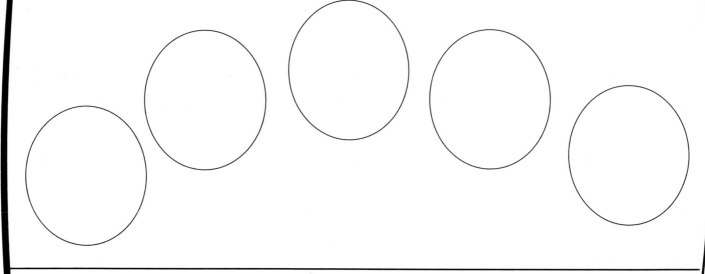

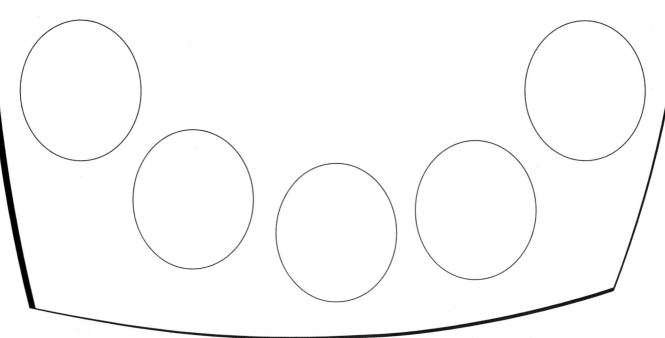

Identifies individual characteristics.

NAME

I am a friend

List three things you like to do with your friends.

1. _____

2. _____

3. _____

List three things your friends like about you.

1. _____

2. _____

3. _____

List two ways you can be helpful to others.

1. _____

2. _____

List two ways your friends can help you.

1. _____

2. _____

Identifies ways people care about and co-operate with others.

NAME

Self-portrait

Draw a picture of yourself. Colour it with your favourite colours. Draw things that you like in the background.

Identifies individual characteristics, likes and dislikes.

Acrostic poem

Write the letters of your first name one under the other down the page. Write a poem, starting each line of the poem with a letter of your name, e.g.,

Always dancing and singing
Loves animals, especially frogs
Is a happy girl

Positive self talk.

NAME

I like me, you like me

Work with a partner.
Write three things you like about yourself.

1. _____

2. _____

3. _____

Ask your friend (or an adult you like) to write three things they like about you.

1. _____

2. _____

3. _____

Compare the two lists. What did you find out about yourself?

Appreciates self and accepts compliments. Gives positive feedback to others.

NAME

Flower power

Write your name in the middle of the flower.
Write something you can do on each petal.
Colour and cut out the flower. Wear it as a
badge or hang it in your room.

Acknowledges individual skills.

NAME

A friendly hand

Write your name across the wrist. Ask five friends or family members to write something they like about you on each finger. Colour and cut out the hand. Hang it in your classroom.

Appreciates self and accepts compliments.

NAME

My friend is special

What is a friend? _____

_____

Choose a friend. List three things that make your friend special.

1. _____

2. _____

3. _____

Show your friend what you have written. Draw yourself and your friend.

Identifies the people and things that are special to them.

NAME

Write a story

Write about something you did or would like to do with a friend – an outing, an adventure, a game...

_____

_____

_____

_____

_____

_____

_____

_____

Identifies the people and things that are special to them.

NAME

Feelings

**Draw lines to link
the faces to the labels.**

happy

sad

angry

surprised

frightened

excited

Write thought balloons
for the faces to tell what
each is thinking about.

Helps identify emotions.

NAME

How would you feel?

Choose a feelings word from the box and write how each person is feeling.

excited	jealous
happy	lonely
sad	angry

Links emotions to expressions and situations.

NAME

Feelings wheel

Colour and cut out the circle and the arrow.
Use a split pin to attach the arrow in the centre of the circle.
Use the feelings wheel during the day to show your feelings.

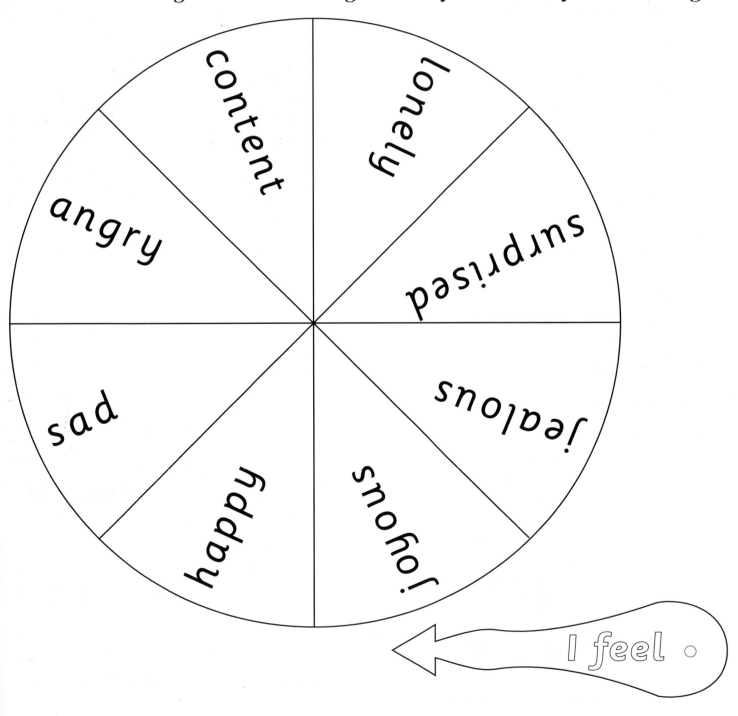

Identifies and expresses personal feelings.

NAME

Let your feelings show

It's OK to show your feelings and to tell others how you are feeling. Sometimes you can just feel the feeling, and sometimes you can also do something about it, e.g., I am sad because my friend won't play with me, so I am going to find someone else to play with.

What things do you get sad about?
Write about or draw them.

Identifies and expresses personal feelings.

NAME

Tell it like it is

Complete the sentences:

I feel happy when _____

_____

I feel angry when _____

_____

I feel sad when _____

_____

I feel relaxed when _____

_____

I feel afraid when _____

_____

I feel joyful when _____

_____

My feelings get hurt when _____

_____

Identifies and expresses personal feelings.

NAME

The best thing ever

Write about or draw the best thing that ever happened to you.

Identifies and expresses personal feelings.

Who said that?

Label the speech bubbles from 1 to 4 to match the right picture.

I am happy because I am going to the beach with my friend.

1

I am cross with myself because I forgot to bring my rock collection for show and tell.

2

I am frightened because a bully said he was going to get me after school.

3

I am sad because mummy said I have to set my tadpoles free.

4

Links emotions to expressions and situations.

How would you feel?

Jenny's friends won't play with her. Circle the words that tell how she feels.

lonely   jealous   miserable   grumpy   delighted

angry   sad   upset   happy   excited

Frank's dog has died. Circle the words that tell how he feels.

lonely   jealous   miserable   grumpy   delighted

angry   sad   upset   happy   excited

Katy's grandma has come to visit. Write five words that tell how she feels.

Joey has been invited to a friend's birthday party. Write five words that tell how he feels.

Identifies possible feeling responses to situations

Feelings faces

Draw faces to show
how you feel when . . .

You fall over.

The teacher praises you
for a job well done.

A bully pushes you over.

You get into
trouble for
something that
you didn't do.

You receive a
present.

Helps express feelings.

NAME

My feet can...

List the things that your feet can do. Write as many action words as you can.

Colour and cut out the foot. Hang it in your classroom.

Identifies and assesses own strengths.

NAME

Which friend for which job?

Which friend would you choose to help you ...

... read a story? _____

... take a message to the head teacher?

_____

... fix a sore knee? _____

... find your lost toy? _____

... make a painting? _____

Identifies ways people care about and co-operate with others.

NAME

My favourite things

Draw or write a list of your favourite things:

Identifies and expresses individual likes and dislikes.

NAME

I don't like it!

Use magazines and art paper to make a collage of lots of things that you don't like.

Finish the sentence. I don't like _____

_____

_____

_____

_____

_____ .

Identifies and expresses individual likes and dislikes.

NAME

Wishing and hoping

What would be the best way to celebrate your birthday? Write about or draw the best birthday ever.

Identifies and communicates individual likes and dislikes.

NAME

Like or dislike

Number the items in order from the ones you like most (number 1) to the ones you like least (number 6).

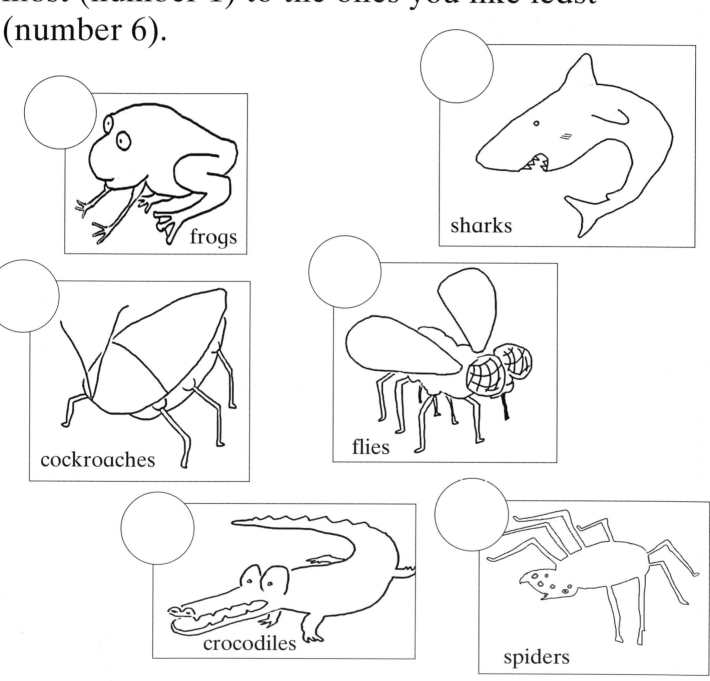

frogs

sharks

cockroaches

flies

crocodiles

spiders

Talk to a partner about your choices.

Identifies and expresses individual likes and dislikes.

NAME

Favourite foods

Draw your favourite food in the boxes.

My favourite breakfast is

My favourite lunch is

My favourite dinner is

My favourite snack is

Identifies and expresses individual likes and dislikes.

NAME

What do you think about...?

Draw faces to show what you think of each school activity. Write a comment if you wish.

reading		
maths		
painting		
drawing		
handwriting		
listening to stories		
PE/sport		

Identifies and expresses feelings and opinions.

Pupil awards

Name _____
Date _____
You should be proud of the way you
_____

_____

_____

Signed _____

Name _____
Date _____
I enjoy having you in my class because
_____

_____

_____

Signed _____

Name _____
Date _____
I value the way
_____

_____

_____

Signed _____

Name _____
Date _____
I am proud of the way
_____

_____

_____

Signed _____

 IDEAS-TO-GO: SELF-ESTEEM — 6-8 © A&C BLACK 2002

CHALLENGES

Me mobiles

What you need:

- wire coat hanger
- magazines, photos, poems and drawings
- string or ribbon
- cardboard
- hole punch
- scissors

What to do:

1. Use the coat hanger to create a mobile about yourself. Attach photos, drawings of yourself, poems, packaging from favourite foods, streamers in your favourite colours, magazine and catalogue pictures of your favourite activities, toys, animals, etc.

2. Write words to describe yourself on cardboard. Cut them out. Use a hole punch to make a hole in the top.

3. Use string to attach them to the mobile.

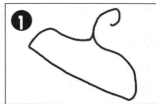

My secret journal

What you need:

- a book to write in
- glue
- various art supplies

What to do:

1. Decorate your book. You could cover it with coloured paper and cut out pictures from magazines of things you like and stick them on, or paste on to it things like feathers or leaves. Or you could cover it with white paper, do drawings on it and colour them in.

2. Do a title page for your book. Write your name on it, so that if you lose it someone can return it to you.

3. Each day, write the date in, then write or draw something in your book. It could be what you did that day, a poem or story, a drawing, or something like a flower stuck in. Try doing this for a week and keep going if you like it. It can be fun to look back and see what you were doing a week ago.

**Paper bag people**

What you need:

- mirror
- a paper plate
- crayons
- paint
- wool, string
- scissors
- magazines and newspapers
- a paper bag
- stapler
- glue, sticky tape
- various other craft materials

What to do:

1. Take a good look at yourself in a mirror and then draw your features (eyes, nose, mouth) on the paper plate. Colour with crayons and then use a paint wash over the whole surface. Attach wool, paper or string for your hair.

2. Paste magazine pictures on to the paper bag and draw pictures of and/or write about things that you like (if you love dogs you could glue pictures of dogs to the bag). Fill the bag with newspaper and then staple the ends together.

3. Staple the paper plate head on to the paper bag body. Make paper legs and arms and staple these to the bag.

4. Hang 'you' up in the classroom.

5. Ask a friend to write a poem about you. Display the poem near your paper bag 'you'.

**Make a puppet**

What you need:

- a paper plate
- scissors
- glue
- sticky tape
- two rulers
- various craft materials

What to do:

1. Use a paper plate to make the puppet's head. Draw features such as eyes, nose, mouth and eyebrows. Attach hair and whatever other decorations you wish, e.g., ribbons, a hat, earrings.

2. Use sticky tape to attach a ruler to the back of the puppet so that you can hold and move the puppet. Attach another ruler across the first to make puppet arms. Hang a piece of fabric over the arms for clothing.

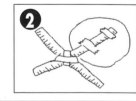

3. Give your puppet a name and introduce your puppet to other puppets and classmates.

TASK CARD 5

Picture Book

the sad pig

What you need:

- picture book
- partner
- friends to act out a story with

What to do:

1. Go to the library to find a picture book in which the characters show their feelings.

2. Read the book with a partner.

3. Choose a number of friends to help you act out the story of the picture book for your class.

4. Ask the class what feelings the characters had, and how they felt about the characters and their situations.

TASK CARD 6

Big bodies

What you need:

- chart paper or large rolls of newsprint paper
- felt tip pens
- paint
- newspaper
- stapler

What to do:

1. Work with one or two friends. One group member should lie down on their back on a sheet of chart paper or newsprint paper. Other group members then trace around the person's body. Trace two copies — one for the front view and one for the back view.

2. Paint the front and back versions of the life size body. Make sure you paint the correct side of each so that when they are stapled together to make the whole body the painted sides face out.

3. Staple the fronts and backs together, decorated side out, filling the inside with scrunched up newspaper as you staple.

4. Write a label for your 'friend', and introduce her/him to the rest of the class, then ask your teacher to hang your 'friend' up.

5. Write a poem about your 'friend' to display with the body.